Cosmic Christmas

Max Lucado

Based in part on a story by

David Lambert

Illustrations by

Greg Dearth

WORD PUBLISHING

Nashville • London • Vancouver • Melbourne

Published by Word Publishing
Nashville, Tennessee

Cosmic Christmas is based in part on a story by David Lambert entitled "Earthward, Earthward, Messenger Bright" which first appeared in the December 1982 issue of *Moody Magazine*. "Earthward, Earthward, Messenger Bright" copyright © 1982, 1990 David Lambert.

Illustrations by Greg Dearth
Design by D[2] DesignWorks

Library of Congress Cataloging-in-Publication data
Lucado, Max
Cosmic Christmas / Max Lucado.
p. cm.
ISBN 0-8499-1530-9 (hardcover)
1. Jesus Christ—Nativity—Fiction. 2. Bible. N.T.—History of Biblical events—Fiction. I. Title.
PS3562.U225C67 1997
813'.54—dc21 97-26523
7890 BVG 4321 CIP

To my Prayer Partners

"The **Word** was God. . . .

the **Word** became a

human and lived

among us."

[John 1:1; 14, NCV]

Cosmic Christmas

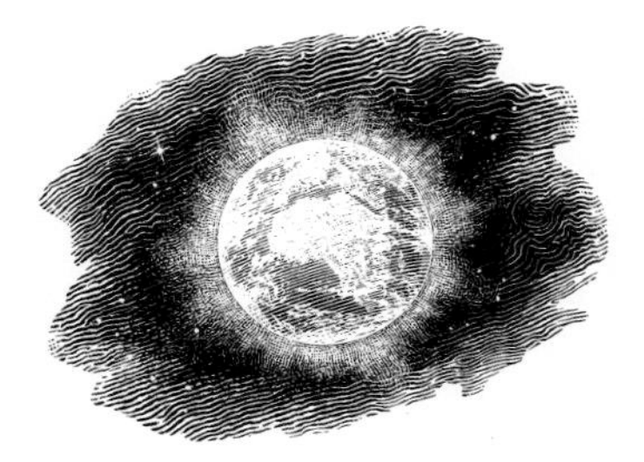

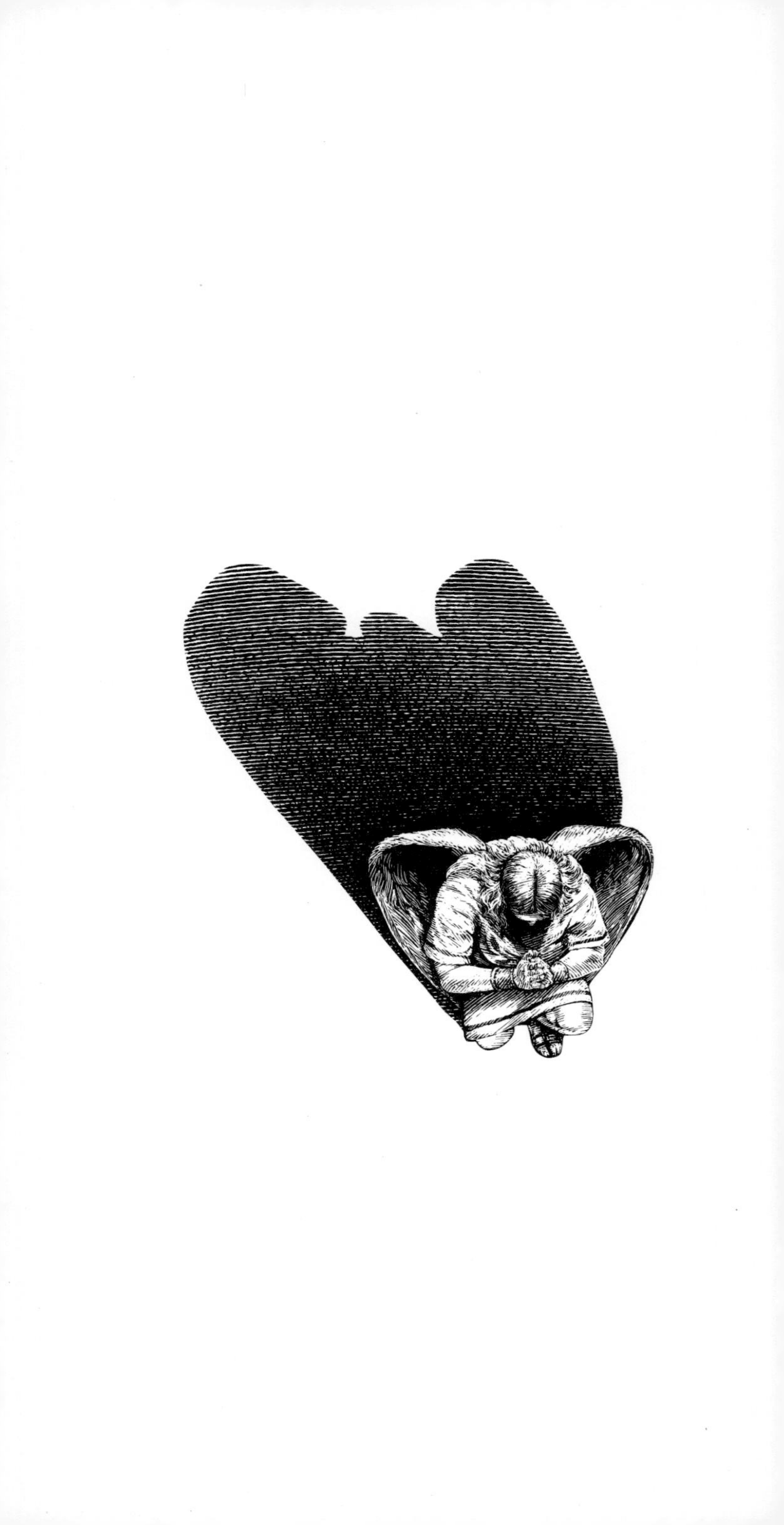

Gabriel."

Just the sound of my King's voice stirred my heart. I left my post at the entryway and stepped into the throne room. To my left was the desk on which sat the Book of Life. Ahead of me was the throne of Almighty God. I entered the circle of unceasing Light, folded my wings before me to cover my face, and knelt before Him. "Yes, my Lord?"

"You have served the kingdom well. You are a noble messenger. Never have you flinched in duty. Never have you flagged in zeal."

I bowed my head, basking in the words. "Whatever You ask, I'll do a thousand times over, my King," I promised.

"Of that I have no doubt, dear messenger." His voice assumed a solemnity I'd never heard Him use. "But your greatest work lies ahead of you. Your next assignment is to carry a gift to Earth. Behold."

I lifted my eyes to see a necklace—a clear vial on a golden chain—dangling from His extended hand.

My Father spoke earnestly, "Though empty, this vial will soon contain My greatest gift. Place it around your neck."

I was about to take it when a raspy voice interrupted me. "And what treasure will You send to Earth this time?"

My back stiffened at the irreverent tone, and my stomach turned at the sudden stench. Such foul odor could only come from one being. I drew my sword and turned to do battle with Lucifer. The Father's hand on my shoulder stopped me.

"Worry not, Gabriel. He will do no harm."

I stepped back and stared at God's enemy. He was completely covered.

A black cassock hung over his skeletal frame, hiding his body and arms and hooding his face. The feet, protruding beneath the robe, were thrice-toed and clawed. The skin on his hands was that of a snake. Talons extended from his fingers. He pulled his cape further over his face as a shield against the Light, but the brightness still pained him. Seeking relief, he turned toward me. I caught a glimpse of a skullish face within the cowl.

"What are you staring at, Gabriel?" he sneered. "Are you that glad to see me?"

I had no words for this fallen angel. Both what I saw and what I remembered left me speechless. I remembered him before the Rebellion: Poised proudly at the vanguard of our force, wings wide, holding forth a radiant sword, he had inspired us to do the same. Who could refuse him? The sight of his velvet hair and coal-black eyes had far outstripped the beauty of any celestial being.

Any being, of course, except our Creator. No one compared Lucifer to God . . . except Lucifer. How he came to think he was worthy of the same worship as God, only God knows. All I knew was that I had not seen Satan since the Rebellion. And what I now saw repulsed me.

I searched for just a hint of his former splendor but saw none.

"Your news must be urgent," spat Satan to God, still unable to bear the Light.

My Father's response was a pronouncement. "The time has come for the second gift."

The frame beneath the cape bounced stiffly as Lucifer chuckled. "The second gift, eh? I hope it works better than the first."

"You're disappointed with the first?" asked the Father.

"Oh, quite the contrary; I've delighted in it." Lifting a bony finger, he spelled a word in the air. C-H-O-I-C-E.

"You gave Adam his choice," Satan scoffed. "And what a choice he made!

He chose me. Ever since the fruit was plucked from the tree in the Garden, I've held Your children captive. They fell. Fast. Hard. They are mine. You have failed. Heh-heh-heh."

"You speak so confidently," replied the Father, astounding me with His patience.

Lucifer stepped forward, his cloak dragging behind him. "Of course! I thwart everything You do! You soften hearts, I harden them. You teach truth, I shadow it. You offer joy, I steal it."

He pivoted and paraded around the room, boasting of his deeds. "The betrayal of Joseph by his brothers—I did that. Moses banished to the desert after killing the Egyptian—I did that. David watching Bathsheba bathe—that was me. You must admit, my work has been crafty."

"Crafty? Perhaps. But effective? No. I know what you will do even before you do it. I used the betrayal of Joseph to deliver My people from famine. Your banishment of Moses became his wilderness training. And yes, David did commit adultery with Bathsheba—but he repented of his sin! And thousands have been inspired by his example and found what he found—unending grace. Your deceptions have only served as platforms for My mercy. You are still My servant, Satan. When will you learn? Your feeble attempts to disturb My work only enable My work. Every act you have intended for evil, I have used for good."

Satan began to growl—a throaty, guttural, angry growl. Softly at first, then louder, until the room was filled with a roar that must have quaked the foundations of hell.

But the King was not bothered. "Feeling ill?"

Lucifer lurked around the room, breathing loudly, searching for words to say and a shadow from which to say them. He finally found the words but never the shadow. "Show me, O King of Light, show me one person on the Earth who always does right and obeys your will."

"Dare you ask? You know there need be only one perfect one, only one sinless one to die for all the others."

"I know Your plans—and You have *failed!* No Messiah will come from Your people. There is none who is sinless. Not one." He turned his back to the desk and began naming the children. "Not Moses. Not Abraham. Not Lot. Not Rebekah. Not Elijah . . ."

The Father stood up from His throne, releasing a wave of holy Light so intense that Lucifer staggered backward and fell. "Those are My children you mock," God's voice boomed. "You think you know much, fallen angel, but you know so little. Your mind dwells in the valley of self. Your eyes see no further than your own needs."

The King walked over and reached for the book. He turned it toward Lucifer and commanded, "Come, Deceiver, read the name of the One who will call your bluff. Read the name of the One who will storm your gates."

Satan rose slowly off his haunches. Like a wary wolf, he walked a wide circle toward the desk until he stood before the volume and read the word: *Immanuel.*

"Immanuel?" he muttered to himself, then spoke in a tone of disbelief. "God with us?" For the first time the hooded head turned squarely toward the face of the Father. "No. Not even You would do that. Not even You would go so far."

"You've never believed Me, Satan."

"But *Immanuel*? The plan is bizarre! You don't know what it is like on Earth!

You don't know how dark I've made it. It's putrid. It's evil. It's . . ."

"It is Mine," proclaimed the King. "And I will reclaim what is Mine. I will become flesh. I will feel what My creatures feel. I will see what they see."

"But what of their sin?"

"I will bring mercy."

"What of their death?"

"I will give life."

Satan stood speechless.

God spoke, "I love My children. Love does not take away the beloved's freedom. But love takes away fear. And Immanuel will leave behind a tribe of fearless children. They will not fear you or your hell."

Satan stepped back at the thought. His retort was childish. "Th-th-they will too!"

"I will take away all sin. I will take away death. Without sin and without death, you have no power."

Around and around in a circle Satan paced, clenching and unclenching his wiry fingers. When he finally stopped, he asked a question that even I was thinking. "Why? Why would You do this?"

The Father's voice was deep and soft. "Because I love them."

The two stood facing each other. Neither spoke. The extremes of the universe were before me. God robed in Light, each thread glowing. Satan canopied in evil, the very fabric of his robe seeming to crawl. Peace contrasting panic. Wisdom confronting foolishness. One able to rescue, the other anxious to condemn.

I have reflected much on what happened next. Though I have relived the moment countless times, I'm as stunned as I was at the first. Never in my wildest thoughts did I think my King would do what He did. Had He demanded Satan's departure, who would have questioned? Had He taken Satan's life, who would have grieved? Had He called me to attack, I would have been willing. But God did none of these.

From the circle of Light came His extended hand. From His throne came an honest invitation. "Will you surrender? Will you return to me?"

I do not know the thoughts of Satan. But I believe that for a fleeting second the evil heart softened. The head cocked slightly, as if amazed that such an offer would be made. But then it yanked itself erect.

"Where will we battle?" he challenged.

The Father sighed at the dark angel's resistance. "On a hill called Calvary."

"If you make it that far." Satan smirked, spinning and marching out the entryway. I watched as his spiny wings extended, and he soared into the heavenlies.

The Father stood motionless for a moment, then turned back to the book.

Opening to the final chapter, He slowly read words I had never heard. No sentences. Just words. Saying each, then pausing:

Jesus,

Nail,

Cross,

Blood,

Tomb,

Life.

He motioned toward me, and I responded, kneeling again before Him. Handing me the necklace, He explained, "This vial will contain the essence of Myself; a Seed to be placed in the womb of a young girl. Her name is

Mary. She lives among My chosen people. The fruit of the Seed is the Son of God. Take it to her."

"But how will I know her?" I asked.

"Don't worry. You will."

I could not comprehend God's plan, but my understanding was not essential. My obedience was. I lowered my head, and He draped the chain around my neck. Amazingly, the vial was no longer empty. It glowed with Light.

"Jesus. Tell her to call My Son *Jesus*."

How thrilling had been our send-off! Michael, the archangel, read to us the words from the Book of Courage. The troops sang to the Father, begging His Spirit to accompany our battalion. The Father rose from His throne in a flood of cascading Light and gave us words of strength.

To the angels He urged, "Be strong, My ministers."

To me He reminded, "Gabriel, Satan desires to destroy the Seed as much as you desire to deliver it. But fear not. I am with you."

"Thy will be done," I resolved and took my place at the apex of the troops. It was time to leave. I began the song of praise to signal our departure. One by one the angels joined me in worship and sang. One final time I faced the Light. We turned and plunged into the heavenlies.

On the wave of His Light we flew. On the crest of our songs we soared. Paragon was at my right, Aegus on my left. Both handpicked by our Father to guard the vial. Ever able. Ever nimble. Ever obedient.

So immense was our number that I could not see its end. Our strength knew no bounds. We flew as a torrent of stars through the universe: I at the helm, thousands of angels behind me. I delighted in a backward glance at the flood of silver wings rising and falling in silent rhythm.

From them came a constant flow of spontaneous praise.

"To God be all glory!"

"Only He is worthy!"

"Mighty is the King of kings and Lord of lords!"

"The battle belongs to God!"

I had chosen only the most able angels

for my company, for only the most able could face the foe. Every angel had been willing, but only the most skilled warriors had been chosen.

We passed the galaxy of Ebon into the constellation of Emmanees. Out of the corner of my eye I caught a glimpse of Exalon, a planet ringed once for every child found faithful to the Father. Through the constellation of Clarion and into the stellar circle of Darius.

Around my neck dangled the glowing vial, its mystery still beyond my understanding.

Behind me I heard the soft voice of Sophio. The Father has gifted him with wisdom, and I have taken him on many journeys. His task is always the same. "Whisper truth to me as we fly," I tell him, and so he does. "Lucifer is the father of lies. There is no truth . . . no truth in him. He comes to steal, kill, and destroy."

As my courage mounted, so did my speed. We knew we would not fail. But we had no idea the battle would come so soon. Only moments across the Ridge of Time, Paragon shouted, "Prepare yourselves!"

Suddenly I was entangled in an invisible net. Row after row of angels tumbled in upon me. Even the final flank was moving too fast to avoid the trap. Within moments, we were a ball of confusion: wings flapping against wings, angels bumping into angels.

Before we could draw our swords, our attackers drew the net so tight we couldn't move. From within the fray I could hear them mocking us.

"*You're* the best of heaven? Ha!"

"To the pit with you!"

"Now you will face the true master!" they taunted.

But their celebration was premature.

The King had prepared me for this web of evil. I knew exactly what to do.

"Holy, Holy, Holy is the Lord God Almighty!" I shouted. "Holy, Holy, Holy is the Lord God Almighty!" Over and over I praised my Master. My angels heard me and joined the worship.

Weakened by the words of truth, the hellhounds released the ropes, allowing us to break free.

"The Lord loves those who praise Him!" Sophio shouted in triumph.

Liberated, we brandished our swords of Light, each connecting with the next, forming a seamless ball of brilliance. Blinded, the demons crashed into each other and then scrambled to escape. I dispatched a platoon to pursue them. "Make sure they don't return!" I instructed.

I studied our flanks—first one side, then the other. No losses. The attack had only increased our resolve. I began to sing, and we resumed our journey, bathed in the Light of our swords and the music of our adoration.

We passed the golden planet, Escholada, signifying our entrance into the chosen galaxy. Each of us knows well these stars. We frequent them on missions. Despite our fond memories of these constellations, we did not pause. Our mission was too vital.

"Gabriel." It was Paragon calling my name. "Behold, in the distance."

I had never seen such a demon. His jackal-like head sat on a long, scaly neck and dragon body. His wings stretched so wide they could engulf a dozen of my fighters. Each of his four feet appeared strong enough to crush an angel. "Who is he?" I asked Paragon and Aegus. It was Sophio who answered.

"It is Phlumar."

"Phlumar? It couldn't be!" Before the Rebellion he was our chief singer and most noble fighter. He would often fly ahead of us, suspended on the graceful rising and falling of lustrous wings.

Many of the songs I now sing, I'd first heard from the lips of Phlumar. *Now look at him,* I thought.

What happened to the sterling eyes and white robe? What happened to the countenance of joy? As I drew near, the repugnant smell of evil caused me to wince. I readied my sword, expecting an attack. I did not expect a question.

"My friend, how long has it been?" the voice was as warm as an archdemon can feign.

"Not long enough, child of hell," I shouted in his face as I soared past. I didn't trust myself to stop. I didn't trust my emotions or my strength. I kept moving, but immediately he was next to me.

"Gabriel, you must listen to me."

"Your prince is a liar and the father of lies."

"But my prince has changed," Phlumar argued.

I did not slow down. Out of the corner of my eye I saw Aegus and Paragon flying wide-eyed with their hands on their swords, awaiting my command. I prayed that they wouldn't see the concern in my eyes. If Phlumar had retained one-tenth of his strength, he would destroy an entire battalion before I could respond. He had been the mightiest in our class.

Phlumar continued, "A miracle has occurred since you left on your mission. My master witnessed your utter defeat of our forces. He is disturbed by your strength and his weakness. He is equally perplexed by the offer of mercy which came in the throne room. He says you were there, Gabriel. Did you see it?"

Though I didn't respond, the image of God's extended hand came to mind. I thought of the tilted head and remembered my first impressions. Could it be that Satan's heart indeed had softened?

Emotion accompanied Phlumar's plea. "Come, Gabriel. Talk with Prince Lucifer.

Plead with him on the Father's behalf. Speak of your Master's love. He will listen to you. Let us go together and urge him to repent."

Phlumar accelerated ahead of me and stopped, forcing me to do the same. He towered above me. I thought I'd prepared for everything, but this I never expected. I prayed for direction.

"Together, Gabriel, you and I together again," the dragon continued. "It can happen. We can be united. Satan's heart is ripe; already mine is changed."

Suddenly it hit me. Again, I knew what to do. I silently thanked God for His guidance.

"Your heart has changed, has it Phlumar?"

His huge head nodded up and down. I turned to Paragon and Aegus. The fear on their faces was giving way to curiosity.

"You long to join our ranks, do you?"

"Yes, Gabriel, I do. The Rebellion was a mistake. Come with me. We will reason with Lucifer. I long to return to heaven. I long to know my former splendor."

By now my plan was clear. "Wonderful news, Phlumar!"

I sensed the surprise on the faces of my angels. "Our God is a good God," I announced. "Slow to anger and quick to forgive. Surely He has heard your confession." I paused and elevated closer to his face and looked into his eyes. "Let us then lift our voices together in praise."

Fear flashed across Phlumar's face. Sophio, perceiving my strategy, announced the truth: "You must worship the Lord your God!"

"But-but-but, I don't remember any of the words."

Realizing Phlumar's true intent, my soldiers began to encircle him. I moved even closer and spoke firmly, "Surely you are willing to worship our Master. Surely you haven't forgotten the songs of worship. Open your mouth and confess the name of the Lord!"

Phlumar looked to the right and left but saw no escape. "Join us," I dared. "If your heart is truly changed, worship with us." I pulled out my sword. "If not, prepare to fight us."

Phlumar knew he'd been foiled. His mouth would not—*could not*—praise the Almighty God. His heart belonged to Satan. He swung his neck to one side, preparing to sweep us into the next galaxy. Had we only *our* strength he would have succeeded. The collective might of our troops could not have resisted his force. But we were empowered from on high. And endued by God's strength, we pounced on the demon in a second.

Before he had a chance to attack, his leathery skin was invaded with swords of Light. It melted like wax. What little flesh still clung to his bones was instantly blotched and infected. Froth fell from his jaws. He opened his mouth and howled a cry as lonely as the skies have heard.

"Kill me," he begged, his voice now husky. He knew any death we gave him would be gracious in comparison to the punishment which awaited him from the hands of Lucifer.

"The angels are kept in bonds for judgment," I reminded him. "Only the Father can kill the eternal." With a twist of our swords we cast this demon of death into the Abyss. For an instant I was sorrowful for this creature. But the sorrow was brief as I remembered how quickly he had followed the prince and his false promises.

I lifted my voice in praise both for our victory and my salvation. I could not help but think of the prophecy the Father spoke to me: "As much as we seek to bring the Seed, so Satan seeks to destroy it."

Lifting hands heavenward, we proclaimed His name above all names as we resumed our journey. Soon we came into the Earth's solar system. I lifted my head as a signal for the army to slow down. The atmosphere of Terra surrounded us, and I searched for the tiny strip of land inhabited by the promised people.

How precious is this globe to Him! I thought. Other orbs are larger. Others grander. But none so suited for Adam and his children. And now the hour of the delivery was at hand. Below me was the small town where God's chosen one slept.

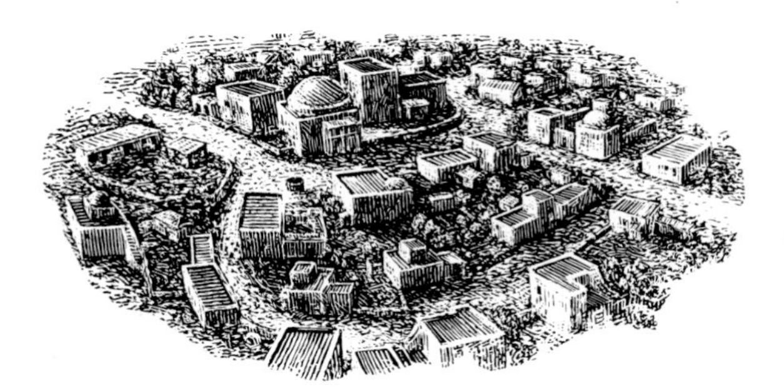

I see you have made it safely."

It was the voice I dreaded. Instantly he was before us. We had no option but to stop.

"You are wearing your old uniform, Lucifer," I accused.

The true angels were entranced at his appearance. As was I. Was this the same devil who had repulsed me in the throne room?

His hoarse whisper was now a vibrant baritone. The skeletal figure now robust and statuesque. Next to his light, our whiteness was gray and dirty. Next to his voice, our voices were but a whimper. We raised our swords, but they flickered like candles against the sun.

My battalions looked upon the devil in confusion. Before the send-off Michael had tried to warn them, but no words prepare you for Lucifer. Without speaking a word, he enchants. Without lifting a weapon, he disarms. Without a touch, he seduces. Angels have been known to follow him without resistance.

But I had the words of the Father in my heart. "He has been a liar since the beginning."

The devil looked at me with a soft smile. "Gabriel, Gabriel. How many times have I spoken your name? My servants can tell you. I have followed you through the years. You are one loyal angel. And now your loyalty is rewarded. The mission of missions."

He threw back his head and laughed, not an evil laugh but a godlike one. *How well he imitates the King!*

"It's no imitation," he said as if he could read my mind. "It's genuine. I rejoice that you have passed our test."

My face betrayed my perplexity.

"Has He not informed you, my friend? How wise is our heavenly Father. How gracious that He should allow me the privilege of telling you. This has been a trial of your loyalty. Your whole mission was a test. The Day of Sorrows. The heavenly Rebellion. The falling of the angels. My visit in the throne room. The net. Phlumar. All of that was to test you, to train you. And now, O Gabriel, the King and I congratulate you. You have proven faithful."

I thought I knew every scheme of Lucifer, every misdeed, every lie. I thought I had anticipated each possible move. I was wrong. This one I never imagined . . . oh, is he sly. He sounded so sincere.

"Do you honestly think I could rebel against God?" he implored. "The Father of Truth? Why, I love Him." His grand voice choked with emotion. "He created me. He gave me free will. And all this time I have worshiped Him from afar so that you could be tested. And, now, my friend, you have passed the Father's test. Why else would He allow you to witness my visit to heaven? It was all a staged event: God's magnum opus to test your dedication."

His words tugged at my breast. My sword dropped to one side and my shield to the other. My thoughts swam. *What is this I feel? What is this power? I know he is evil, yet I find myself weakening. I, at once, long to love and kill him, to trust and deny him.* I turned to look at Aegus and Paragon. They, too, had dropped their weapons, their faces softening as they began to believe the words the Deceiver spoke. Behind them, our armies were relaxing. One by one the swords were dimming. Incredible. With only a few words Lucifer could harness legions. *Is this really true? He looks and sounds so much like the Father . . .*

All of us were beginning to fall under his control.

All, that is, except one. In the distance I saw Sophio. His eyes were not on Lucifer. He was looking heavenward. I could hear his declaration, mounting in volume with each phrase. "Neither death, nor life, neither angels nor demons, neither the present nor the future, nor any powers, neither height nor depth nor anything else in all creation, will be able to separate us from the love of God!"

Sophio's prayer was a beam into the sky. With my eyes I followed the shaft of Light. At its end I could see my

Father standing. One glimpse of His glory and my confusion cleared. I snapped erect and repositioned my shield. Lucifer, for the first time, saw Sophio praying. His smile vanished, then he forced it to return.

He spoke faster, but the true rasp of his voice was returning. "The Father awaits us, Gabriel. Let us smash the vial in celebration of the Father's victory. Let us return with joy. Your mission is complete. You will be rewarded with a throne like mine. You will be like God."

If Satan had any chance, he just lost it. "Liar!" I defied. "I have heard those words before. I have heard that promise.

It is a lie, and you are the father of lies. You stink, you buzzard. To hell with you!"

Though I knew my sword would not stop Lucifer, still I unsheathed my weapon. "Almighty God, save us!" I prayed. He did. My sword projected a Light far greater than ever before—a Light so bright that Lucifer covered his eyes and released a deluge of curses.

I turned to my angels; they were again alert and poised, the spell broken and their courage restored. They lifted their swords in defiance. The ever-increasing Light illuminated the devil, revealing what I had seen in the throne room, only now his hood lay back. The skullish face violated the sky.

I drove my Light into the devil's heart. As I did, Aegus did the same from the other side. Satan screamed, writhing in pain as our Lights fused in purging heat. From within him scampered the ogres of a thousand miseries: loneliness, anger, fear.

In one final, desperate attempt, Lucifer twisted toward me and lunged at heaven's vial. He never had a chance. Paragon's sword swept out of the sky, severing Satan's hand from his arm, sending it spiraling into the night. A wave of stench forced us to lift our shields before our faces. Satan threw back his head, his visage contorted in pain. The voice which only moments before had charmed, now hissed.

"I'll be back!" Lucifer swore. "I'll be back."

Sophio shook his head in disgust. "Disguised as an angel of Light...," he said softly.

As quickly as he had appeared, Satan was gone. And we erupted in praise.

"Holy, holy, holy is the Lord God Almighty!"

"King of kings and Lord of lords!"

As the Father received our praise, He whispered to me. I heard Him as if at my side. "Go, Gabriel; go and tell Mary."

On a wave of worship I flew, this time alone. I circled through the clouds and over the ground. Below me was the city where Mary was born. The Father was right; I knew her in an instant. Her heart had no shadow. Her soul was as pure as any I've seen.

I made the final descent. "Mary." I kept my voice low so as not to startle her.

She turned but saw nothing. Then I realized I was invisible to her. I waved my wings before my body and incarnated. She covered her face at the Light and shrank into the protection of the doorway.

"Don't be afraid," I urged.

The minute I spoke, she looked up toward the sky. Again I was amazed.

I praised my Father for His wisdom. Her heart is so flawless, so willing. "Greetings. God be with you."

Her eyes widened, and she turned as if to run. "Mary, you have nothing to fear. You have found favor with God.

You will become pregnant and give birth to a son and call His name Jesus. He will be great. He will be called the Son of the Highest. The Lord God will give Him the throne of His father David; He will rule Jacob's house forever—no end, ever, to His kingdom."

Though she was listening, she was puzzled.

"But how? I've never slept with a man."

Before I spoke I looked up into the heavens. The Father was standing, giving me His blessing.

I continued, "The Holy Spirit will come upon you, the power of the highest hover over you; therefore, the child you bring to birth will be called Holy, Son of God. Nothing, you see, is impossible with God."

Mary looked at me then up into the sky. For a long time she gazed into the blueness, so long that I, too, looked up. Did she see the angels? Did the heavens open? I do not know. But I do know when I looked back at her, she was smiling.

"Yes, I see it all now: I'm the Lord's maid, ready to serve. Let it be with me just as you say."

As she spoke, a Light appeared in her womb. I glanced at the vial. It was empty.

Joseph led the donkey off the side of the road and rubbed his hand over his forehead. "Let's find a place to spend the night. It'll be dark before we reach Bethlehem."

Mary didn't respond. Joseph walked around the side of the animal and looked into his wife's face. She was asleep! Chin on her chest, hands on her stomach. How had she been able to doze off while riding on the back of a donkey?

Suddenly her head popped up and her eyes opened. "Are we there?"

"No," smiled the young husband. "We still have several hours to go. I see an inn up ahead. Shall we spend the night?"

"Oh, Joseph. I'm feeling we should continue until we reach Bethlehem."

Then she paused. "Perhaps we can stop for a rest."

He sighed, smiled, squeezed her hand, and resumed his place, leading the donkey toward the simple structure on the side of the road. "It's crowded," Joseph said as he lowered Mary to the ground. It took several minutes for Joseph to find a bench where the two could sit.

"I'll return in a moment with something to eat."

Joseph elbowed his way through the crowd. He turned around in time to see a woman take his empty seat next to Mary. Mary started to object, but then she smiled, looked through the crowd at Joseph, and shrugged.

Not an unkind bone in her body, he mused.

Of all the bizarre events over the last few months, he was sure of one thing: the heart of his wife. He'd never met anyone like her. Her story that an angel appeared in the middle of the afternoon? Could have been some kid playing a trick. His memory of an angel appearing in his sleep? Could have been from God . . . could have been from too much wine. Her story about her uncle being struck speechless until the cousin was born? Could have been laryngitis.

But her story about being a pregnant virgin? Mary doesn't lie. She's as pure as an angel. So if Mary says she's a virgin, she is. If she says the baby is the Son of God, let's just hope He gets His nose from the Father's side of the family.

Mary—round-faced and short—wasn't a beauty by any means. A bit hefty even before she was pregnant. But her eyes always twinkled, and her heart was bigger than the Mediterranean. She had an ever-present smile and the countenance of a person about to deliver the punch line of a good joke. That's what made Mary, Mary. Joseph shook his head as Mary pushed herself to her feet so the husband of the woman who'd taken Joseph's seat could sit down.

The man started to object, but she waved him off. "I need to stand for a minute," she mouthed to Joseph as she walked in his direction. Or waddled in his direction. They'd both hoped the baby would come in Nazareth; at least they had family there. They knew no one in Bethlehem.

Joseph tucked her arm in his, and the two leaned against a wall. "You sure you want to go farther?"

She nodded, and after more than a few "excuse me's" and "pardon me's," the two found their way to the door.

"One more drink of water?" Mary asked.

"Of course. Wait outside."

Mary leaned against a tree as Joseph stood in line at the well. She smiled at the way he quickly struck up a conversation with the man in front of him. When he returned carrying water, the man came with him.

"Mary, this is Simon. He's also going to Bethlehem and has offered us a place to sit in his ox cart."

"That's kind of you."

"I'd enjoy the company. Just tie your donkey to the back," Simon smiled.

"Excuse me. I heard you say Bethlehem.

Would you have room for one more?"

The request came from an old man with a long silver beard and the fringes of a rabbi. Simon quickly nodded.

After helping Mary into the wagon, Joseph turned to help the rabbi. "What was your name?"

"Gabriel," I answered, and took a seat across from Mary.

Aegus hovered in front of the wagon and Paragon behind. Both were alert, wings spread and swords drawn. Up until the stop at the inn, I had flown with them. But something seemed suspicious about the wagon, so I took the form of a person. I quickly regretted not having chosen the appearance of a young merchant. (The beard I wore itched horribly.)

My battalion didn't need me to remind them, but I did anyway. "Hell does not want Immanuel born. Stay alert." Invisible angels a dozen deep encircled the wagon. I smiled to myself. Simon could have driven blindfolded. There was no way this cart would have failed to reach its destination.

The congested road slowed our progress. We traveled no faster than those around us on foot, but at least Mary could rest. She closed her eyes and leaned her head against the side of the wagon. I could see the radiance in her womb. He glowed like a healing fire. I worshiped Him, even unborn. My heart celebrated with silent songs of praise which He could hear. I smiled as Mary felt Him move. Around me the army heard my song and joined in praise.

About an hour later I sensed it. Evil. My body tensed. The feel of deviltry was on the road, lurking among the travelers. I alerted the angels. "Be ready." Sophio entered the cart and whispered, "He prowls as a lion, looking for someone to devour." I nodded in agreement and searched the faces of those walking near the wagon.

A young man approached the cart. He asked Mary, "You look tired. Would you like some water?" Mary said, "Thank you," and reached for the offered wine-skin. I jumped to my feet, purposefully bumping the demon's arm. The water pouch fell to the ground as Mary and Joseph heard me apologize. Only the young man heard me challenge him: "Beast of hell, you shall not touch this daughter of God."

The demon vacated the body of the man and drew a sword. "You have no chance this time, Gabriel," he cried, and suddenly dozens of demons appeared from all sides and raced toward Mary.

"Joseph," she spoke, her face full of pain as she held her womb,"something's wrong. It—it's like something's hitting me in the stomach. I'm in terrible pain."

Instantly I assumed angelic form and wrapped myself around her as a shield. The demons' swords pierced me. I felt their sting—but she was safe. Just then Paragon and seven angels appeared, slashing at the demons' backs. The demons were distracted but determined.

The wagon began to shake. Travelers began to panic. I heard a cry. I looked up in time to see Simon clutch his throat. His face was red, and his eyes bulged. Around his neck I could see the spiny fingers of a troll. Another demon had bewitched the ox, causing it to lurch spastically toward the side of the road.

Someone screamed, "Stop the wagon, there's a cliff ahead!"

A courageous man attempted to grab the reins, but he couldn't move. Afterward he told people he was frozen with fear. I knew otherwise: A demon had webbed him to the road.

Simon gasped for breath and slumped sideways on the seat. I knew he was dead. The possessed animal swerved madly toward the cliff. I looked at Mary. Joseph's arm was around her shoulders; her hand was on her round stomach. I knew that in a matter of seconds we

would crash over the edge into the valley below. The driver was dead; the wagon was out of control. I turned and prayed to the only One who could help.

From the womb, He spoke. His parents did not hear. The word was not for the ears of Mary and Joseph. Only the hosts of heaven and hell could hear the word. And when they did, all stopped.

"Life!"

The command flooded the wagon as totally as it had flooded Eden. The demons began scattering like rats. "Life!" came the command a second time. Simon coughed as air filled his lungs. "The reins!" I shouted. He gasped, grabbed the reins, and pulled himself erect. Through watery eyes he saw the edge of the road and instinctively yanked the animal back until it stopped. We were safe.

But even with the demons gone, I took no chances. My command to Sophio was urgent. "They found her on the road; they will find her room at the inn. Do what needs to be done." Sophio saluted and soared ahead to the inn at Bethlehem.

Mary remained enveloped in my Light. Joseph watched her with alarm; she relaxed in my care. "I'm better now," she said. "What happened to the rabbi?"

But don't you have just one room?" Joseph pleaded.

"To be honest, I did. But only moments ago a large delegation arrived and took every last bed. I don't have a place for you and your wife."

Joseph tried to be patient, but his jaw was tightening. He leaned forward so his face was inches from the innkeeper's. "See that lady in the cart?"

he asked through his teeth. "She is my wife. She could deliver any minute. She nearly had the baby this afternoon in a wagon. She is in pain right now. Do you want the baby to be born here in your doorway?"

"No, of course not, but I can't help you. Please understand. I have no more rooms."

"I heard you, but it is midnight and cold. Don't you have any place for us to keep warm?"

The man sighed, looked at Mary and then at Joseph. He walked into his house and returned with a lamp. "Behind the inn is a trail which will lead you down a hill. Follow it until you come to a stable. It's clean, at least as clean as stables usually are." With a shrug he added, "You'll be warm there."

Joseph couldn't believe what he was hearing. "You expect us to stay in the stable?"

"Joseph." It was Mary speaking. She'd heard every word. He turned; she was smiling. He knew exactly what the smile meant. Enough arguing.

His sigh puffed his cheeks. "That will be fine," Joseph consented and took the lamp.

"Strange," the clerk muttered to himself as the couple left. Turning to his wife he asked, "Who was the man who took all the rooms?"

Opening the register, the woman read the name aloud. "Different name. Sophio. Must be Greek."

e were a wreath of Light around the stable, a necklace of diamonds around the structure. Every angel had been called from his post for the coming, even Michael. None doubted God would, but none knew how He could, fulfill His promise.

"I've heated the water!"

"No need to yell, Joseph, I hear you fine."

Mary would have heard had Joseph whispered. The stable was even smaller than Joseph had imagined, but the innkeeper was right—it was clean. I started to clear out the sheep and cow, but Michael stopped me. "The Father wants all of creation to witness the moment."

"Aaaiieee!"

Mary gripped Joseph's arm with one hand and a feed trough with the other. The thrust in her abdomen lifted her back, and she leaned forward.

"Is it time?" Joseph panted.

She shot back a glance, and he had his answer.

Within moments the Awaited One was born. I was privileged to have a position close to the couple, only a step behind Michael. We both gazed into the wrinkled face of the infant. Joseph had placed hay in a feed trough, giving Jesus His first bed.

All of God was in the infant. Light encircled His face and radiated from His tiny hands. The very glory I had witnessed in His throne room now burst through His skin.

I felt we should sing but did not know what. We had no song. We had no verse. We had never seen the sight of God in a baby. When God had made a star, our words had roared. When He had delivered His servants, our tongues had flown with praise. Before His throne, our songs never ended.

But what do you sing to God in a feed trough?

In that moment a wonderful thing happened. As we looked at the baby Jesus, the darkness lifted. Not the darkness of

the night, but the darkness of the mystery. Heaven's enlightment engulfed the legions.

Our minds were filled with Truth we had never before known. We became aware for the first time of the Father's plan to rescue those who bear His name. He revealed to us all that was to come. At once amazed and stunned, the eye of every angel went to one part of the child: the hands which would be pierced. "At the pounding of the nail," God told us, "you will not save Him. You will watch, you will hear, you will yearn, but you will not rescue."

Paragon and Aegus turned to me, begging for an explanation. I had none.

I exist to serve my King and I must watch Him be tortured? I looked to Michael; his face was stone-hard with torment. I recognized the look, for I felt the same. We could not fathom the command. "How will we sit silent as You suffer?" we asked in unison.

There was no response.

Sophio was whispering. I drew near to hear his words:

"A child has been given to us; God has given a Son to us. He will be responsible for leading the people. His name will be

Wonderful Counselor,

Powerful God,

Father Who Lives Forever,

Prince of Peace.

He will be wounded for the wrong they did, crushed for the evil they did. The punishment which will make them well will be given to Him. They will be healed because of His wounds."

Once again, I heard the words I had heard first in the throne room. Only this time, I understood.

Jesus

Nail

Cross

Blood

Tomb

Life

S*o this is He. Immanuel. So this is God's gift. A Savior. He shall save His people from their sins.* "Worthy is the Lamb," I whispered, as I knelt before my God. My heart was full. I turned to Mary as she cradled her child and I spoke. It didn't matter that she couldn't hear me. The stars could. All of nature could. And most of all, my King could.

"Do you know who you hold, Mary? You secure the Author of grace. He who is ageless is now moments old. He who is limitless is now suckling your milk. He who strides upon the stars, now has legs too weak to walk; the hands which held the oceans are now an infant's fist. To

Him who has never asked a question, you will teach the name of the wind. The Source of language will learn words from you. He who has never stumbled, you will carry. He who has never hungered, you will feed. The King of creation is in your arms."

"What manner of love is this?" Michael whispered, and again we were covered with silence. A blanket of awe. Finally, Michael again opened his mouth, this time to sing. He began quietly, pausing between the words.

"Glory,

glory,

glory to God in the highest."

One by one we joined. "Glory,

glory,

glory to God in the highest."

Gradually the chorus grew louder and faster: "Glory, glory to God in the highest. Glory, glory to God in the highest. Glory, glory to God in the highest."

Our praise rose into the realms of the universe. In the most distant galaxy the dust on the oldest star danced with our praise. In the depths of the ocean, the water rippled with adoration. The tiniest microbe turned, the mightiest constellation spun, all of nature joined with us as we worshiped Immanuel, the God who had become flesh.

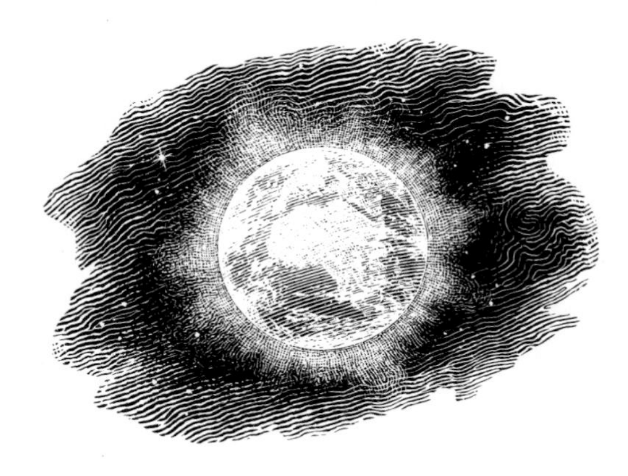

Afterword

Christmas is full of cozy thoughts: a sleeping Jesus, wide-eyed shepherds, a soft-faced Mary. The nativity sentiment is warm, the emotion is joy, and the feeling is peace. Such is the picture in the gospels of Matthew and Luke. In John's Book of Revelation, however, he offers another perspective. From his perspective, the birth of Jesus stirs more than excitement; it stirs evil.

Pulling back the curtain of the skies, he reveals a bloody war in the heavens. John sees a woman, ready to give birth. He sees a dragon, ready to bring death. The woman is beautiful and the dragon ugly. The dragon lunges at the newborn child, but he is too late. The child and the mother are granted safety and then "there was a war in heaven. Michael and his angels fought against the dragon, and the dragon and his angels fought back" (Rev. 12:7 NIV).

"A war in heaven." I've wondered about that war: when it occurred, who it involved, what it meant. *Cosmic Christmas* is the result of those wonderings.

Several colleagues have stirred my imagination. Eugene Peterson stretched me through his study of the Book of Revelation, *Reversed Thunder*. Some time ago I read an article by Philip Yancey which broadened my thinking ("Cosmic Combat," *Christianity Today*, December 12, 1994). I am indebted to the creative pen of David Lambert for his story, "Earthward, Earthward, Messenger Bright." This piece, which appeared in the December, 1982 issue of *Moody Monthly*, offered a fresh, creative approach to the Christmas story. That approach sparked with this writer and led ultimately to the development of *Cosmic Christmas*.

I'm equally appreciative to Steve Green, Karen Hill, Liz Heaney and the wonderful team at Word for your incredible support.

Parts of *Cosmic Christmas* are fiction—fruits of my imagination. Other parts of the story, however, are true. Whether or not you like the fiction is insignificant. But whether or not you see the truth is essential.

Scripture, for example, says nothing of a vial containing the essence of Christ, an arch demon named Phlumar, an angel named Sophio, or several of the other characters and events about which you just read. Scripture is, however, very clear that "our fight is not against people on earth but against the rulers and authorities and the powers of this world's darkness, against the spiritual powers of evil in the heavenly world" (Eph. 6:12 NCV).

The Bible doesn't refer to angels trapped in nets or Satan sweet-talking Gabriel. The Bible is clear, though, that Satan is real and his life purpose is to "be like God Most High" (Isa.14:14).

God's creation is divided into two camps: those who follow God and those who follow Satan. Satan is the energizing power of the unsaved (Eph.2:2) and God is the energizing power of the saved (Phil. 2:13). The saved are to live aware of, but not afraid of Satan. The devil prowls about as a lion looking for someone to devour (1 Pet.5:8). But the believer need not live in horror, because "greater is he who is in you, than he that is in the world" (I John 4:4 KJV). We must put on the armor of God to fight against "the devil's evil tricks" (Eph. 6:11) and remember that Satan disguises himself as "an angel of light" (II Cor. 11:13).

Our weapons against Satan are the same as those used by Gabriel and the angelic army: prayer, praise, truth, and trust. We do not rely upon our own strength, but upon God's. "So stand strong, with the belt of truth tied around your waist and the protection of right living on your chest. On your feet wear the Good News of peace to help you stay strong. And also use the shield of faith with which you can stop all the burning arrows of the Evil One. Accept God's salvation as your helmet, and take the sword of the Spirit, which is the word of God. Pray in the Spirit at all times . . . (Eph. 6:14-18).

Finally, the Bible tells no story of a throne room encounter where Lucifer is offered a second chance. But the Bible does contain page after page showing God giving grace to the scallywags and turncoats of the world. He seems more willing to give grace than we are to seek it. Such divine love leaves me to wonder one thing more: if the old snake himself sought mercy, wouldn't he, too, find it where millions have—at the foot of the cross of Christ?

John's description of the "war in the heavens" doesn't answer all our questions, but it does answer the most important. He tells us who won. God did. He also tells us who matters. You do. Imagine, if God will fight such a fight to save you . . . He must really think you are worth the effort. Though we may wonder about the war that occurred, there is no need to wonder about His love . . . He really cares about His children.

Merry (Cosmic) Christmas!